SEE IT GROW!
See a Pumpkin Grow

by Kirsten Chang

BELLWETHER MEDIA • MINNEAPOLIS, MN

T0018876

Blastoff! Readers are carefully developed by literacy experts to build reading stamina and move students toward fluency by combining standards-based content with developmentally appropriate text.

 Level 1 provides the most support through repetition of high-frequency words, light text, predictable sentence patterns, and strong visual support.

 Level 2 offers early readers a bit more challenge through varied sentences, increased text load, and text-supportive special features.

 Level 3 advances early-fluent readers toward fluency through increased text load, less reliance on photos, advancing concepts, longer sentences, and more complex special features.

★ **Blastoff! Universe**

Reading Level

Grade
K

Grades
1–3

Grade
4

This edition first published in 2023 by Bellwether Media, Inc.

No part of this publication may be reproduced in whole or in part without written permission of the publisher. For information regarding permission, write to Bellwether Media, Inc., Attention: Permissions Department, 6012 Blue Circle Drive, Minnetonka, MN 55343.

Library of Congress Cataloging-in-Publication Data

LC record for See a Pumpkin Grow available at http://lccn.loc.gov/2022039508

Editor: Betsy Rathburn   Designer: Brittany McIntosh

Printed in the United States of America, North Mankato, MN.

Table of Contents

On the Vine

Pumpkins are big, orange fruits.
They grow on **vines**.

vine

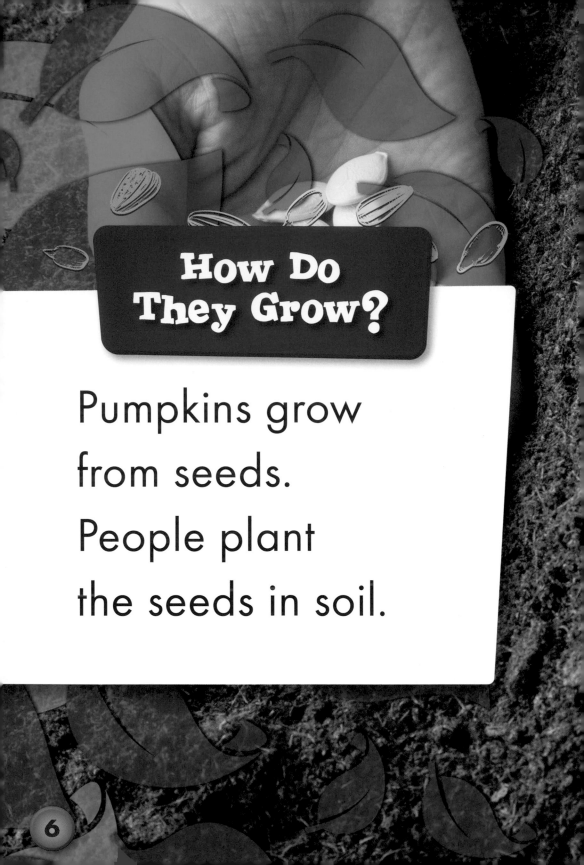

How Do They Grow?

Pumpkins grow from seeds. People plant the seeds in soil.

**planting
seeds**

Seeds need water.
They grow roots.
They **sprout**.

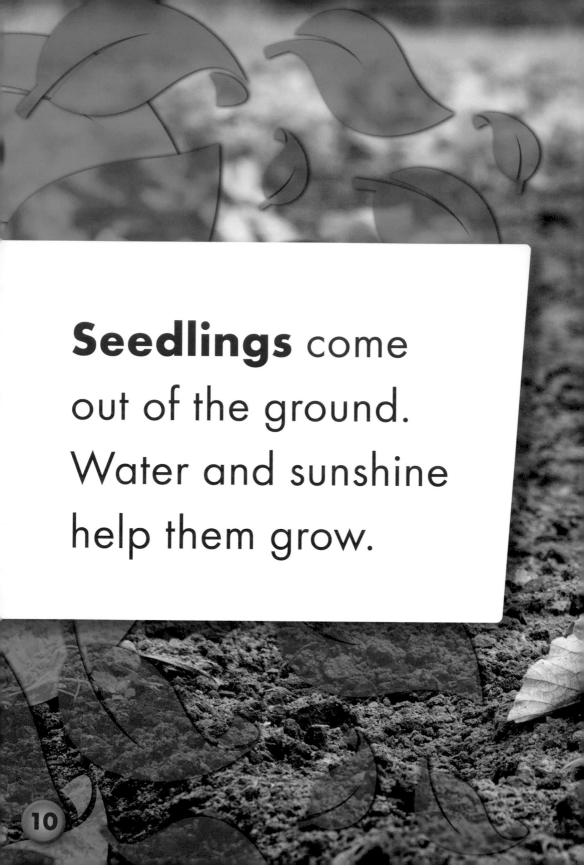

Seedlings come out of the ground. Water and sunshine help them grow.

Needed to Grow

soil | water | sunshine

seedling

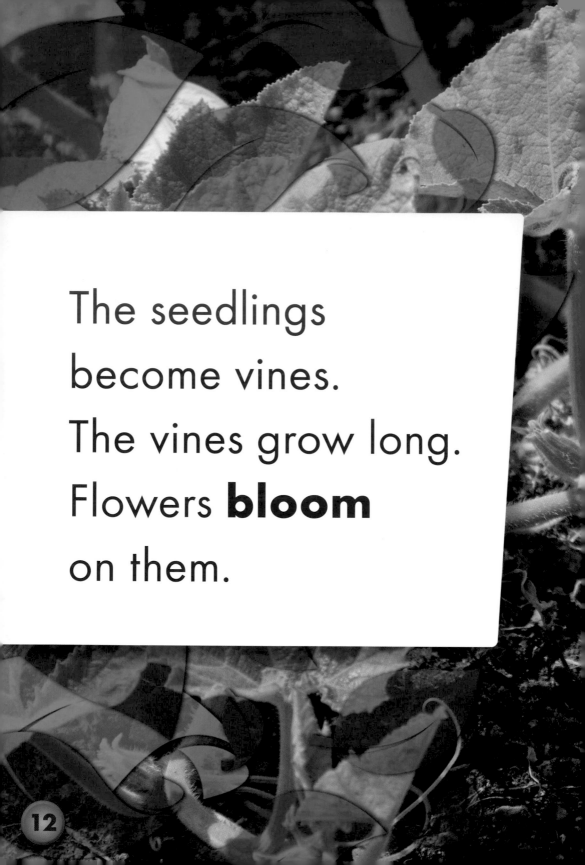

The seedlings become vines. The vines grow long. Flowers **bloom** on them.

flower

vine

13

Bees **pollinate** the flowers. The flowers grow into small, green pumpkins.

bee
pollinating
flower

In about three months,
they grow big!
They turn orange
as the weather cools.

Fully Grown

People pick pumpkins. They use the seeds to grow more pumpkins!

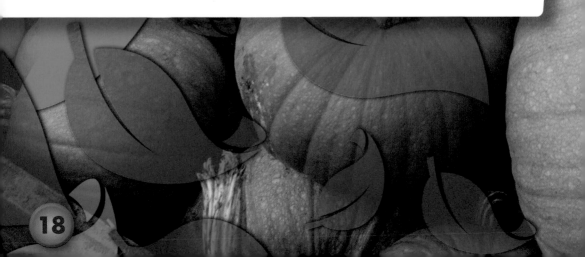

Pumpkin Life Cycle

1 seeds are planted in soil

2 seeds grow vines and flowers

3 bees pollinate flowers

4 pumpkins grow and seeds form

We **carve** pumpkins and bake pies. Pumpkins are used for food and fun!

Using Pumpkins

pumpkin pie

roasted pumpkin seeds

carved pumpkins

carved pumpkins

21

Glossary

bloom

to make flowers

seedlings

small, young plants

carve

to cut in a special pattern

sprout

to grow from a seed

pollinate

to give pollen to make seeds grow

vines

the long, thin stems of some plants

To Learn More

AT THE LIBRARY

Black, Sonia W. *Seed to Pumpkin*. New York, N.Y.: Children's Press, 2021.

Grack, Rachel. *Pumpkin Seed to Pie*. Minneapolis, Minn.: Bellwether Media, 2020.

Peters, Katie. *Let's Look at Pumpkins*. Minneapolis, Minn.: Lerner Publications, 2021.

ON THE WEB

FACTSURFER

Factsurfer.com gives you a safe, fun way to find more information.

1. Go to www.factsurfer.com.

2. Enter "see a pumpkin grow" into the search box and click 🔍.

3. Select your book cover to see a list of related content.

Index

The images in this book are reproduced through the courtesy of: Nataly Studio, front cover (seed); Werner Muenzker, front cover (young pumpkin); topseller, front cover (pumpkin), p. 3; Harmony Video Production, pp. 4-5; Anna solovei/ Alamy, pp. 6-7; chinahbzyg, pp. 8-9; ANDA MIKELSONE/ Alamy, pp. 10-11; Nik Merkulov, p. 11 (top left); Jurga Jot, p. 11 (top middle); photolinc, p. 11 (top right); suprabhat, pp. 12-13; Peter Turner Photography, pp. 14-15; Davide Bonora, pp. 15 (top), 22 (pollinate); J. Ruscello/ Alamy, pp. 16-17; Sun_Shine, pp. 18-19; Rusty Dodson, pp. 20-21; melei5, p. 21 (top left); A_M_Radul, p. 21 (top middle); Yellowj, p. 21 (top right); Andrei Azanfirei, p. 22 (bloom); alexkich, p. 22 (carve); martin.dlugo, p. 22 (seedlings); GOLFX, p. 22 (sprout); jianbing Lee, p. 22 (vines); MIGUEL G. SAAVEDRA, p. 23.